Did Plate Tectonics Give Rise to Life?

Unraveling Earth's Deepest Mystery

Authored by

Zahid Ameer

Published by

Goodword eBooks

ISBN: 9798300021580

DEDICATION

"I dedicate this book to my beloved parents, whose wisdom I hold in the highest regard. Their every word of guidance has been a beacon of light, illuminating the path of my life and shaping the essence of who I am."

Did Plate Tectonics Give Rise to Life?

Contents:

Did Plate Tectonics Give Rise to Life?

Introduction:

The Earth is a living, dynamic planet, constantly reshaping itself through powerful geological forces that have been at work for over 4.5 billion years. Of all these processes, plate tectonics is one of the most crucial and far-reaching. Plate tectonics, the slow but steady movement of the Earth's lithospheric plates, is responsible for the shifting of continents, the rise and fall of mountain ranges, the opening and closing of oceans, and the seismic activity that frequently reshapes our planet's surface. However, the impact of plate tectonics reaches far deeper than just the landforms and geological features that we can observe. Beneath the surface, plate tectonics may have played an essential and previously underappreciated role in the origin and evolution of life on Earth.

This book seeks to explore one of the most profound questions in Earth science and biology: did plate tectonics give rise to life? In other words, could the Earth's unique tectonic processes have created the conditions necessary for life to emerge, evolve, and flourish? While many aspects of Earth's early history remain a mystery, there is growing evidence that the movement and interaction of tectonic plates played a critical role in fostering life's development.

The Interconnection Between Geology and Biology

At first glance, the connection between geology and biology may not seem obvious. Geology typically deals with the physical structure and processes of the Earth, whereas biology focuses on living organisms. Yet, the two are intricately linked. Earth's geological activity has continuously shaped the environments where life exists, while life has, in turn, impacted geological processes. For instance, plate tectonics drives the carbon cycle, a fundamental process that helps regulate Earth's climate, making the planet habitable for life as we know it. It also forms the ocean basins and mountain ranges, which create diverse ecosystems and habitats for different species.

To understand the relationship between plate tectonics and the origin of life, we must delve into the Earth's deep history. The early Earth was a harsh and unstable place. Volcanoes spewed gases into the atmosphere, comets and asteroids bombarded the surface, and the planet's crust was still in the process of solidifying. During this time, about 3.5 to 4 billion years ago, the first signs of life began to appear in the form of simple, microscopic organisms. But how could life emerge in such a tumultuous environment? The answer may lie in the unique conditions created by the movement of Earth's tectonic plates.

The Origins of Plate Tectonics and Early Earth

Did Plate Tectonics Give Rise to Life?

One of the defining characteristics of Earth, as opposed to other planets in our solar system, is the presence of plate tectonics. While Venus and Mars may have had some tectonic activity in the past, Earth is the only planet where active plate tectonics have been continuously operating for billions of years. This movement of plates has shaped Earth's surface in ways that are not only visually stunning but also vital to the sustenance of life. It is believed that Earth's tectonic plates began forming relatively early in the planet's history, but it wasn't until the Archean Eon, roughly 2.5 to 4 billion years ago, that they began to move and interact in the way we understand today.

The onset of plate tectonics had far-reaching consequences for Earth's development, particularly for the creation of stable landmasses and the regulation of the planet's internal heat. Volcanic activity driven by tectonics released gases that helped to form Earth's early atmosphere. Additionally, plate tectonics created new environments like mid-ocean ridges and hydrothermal vent systems, which provided not only the building blocks of life but also a steady supply of chemical energy in the form of mineral-rich water— possibly where life first emerged.

The Role of Hydrothermal Vents and Early Life

One of the most compelling hypotheses about the origin of life focuses on hydrothermal vents, which are found along tectonic boundaries in the deep ocean. These vents are formed when seawater seeps into cracks in the Earth's crust, is heated by underlying magma, and then spews back into the ocean, laden with minerals and heat. This process creates a unique environment that is rich in chemicals like hydrogen sulfide, methane, and iron, which certain primitive life forms can use to generate energy in the absence of sunlight.

The discovery of extremophiles—organisms that can survive in extreme environments, such as those found around hydrothermal vents—has lent credence to the idea that life could have originated in such environments. In the darkness of the deep ocean, far from the sun's energy, these organisms thrive by relying on the heat and chemicals provided by tectonic activity. This discovery has revolutionized our understanding of where and how life can exist and suggests that plate tectonics may have provided the conditions necessary for life to begin on Earth.

Plate Tectonics and the Earth's Climate

Another critical way in which plate tectonics may have contributed to the development of life is through the regulation of Earth's climate. Tectonic activity plays a key role in the carbon cycle, which regulates the amount of carbon dioxide (CO_2) in the atmosphere. This process helps control the Earth's temperature and has contributed to maintaining the "Goldilocks" conditions that make our planet habitable—not too hot and not too cold.

Volcanoes, driven by tectonic forces, release CO_2 into the atmosphere, contributing to the greenhouse effect that warms the planet. However, plate tectonics also enables the removal of CO_2 from the atmosphere over long timescales. When tectonic plates subduct—meaning one plate moves beneath another—carbon-containing minerals are dragged into the Earth's mantle, effectively sequestering CO_2. Over millions of years, this delicate balance of CO_2 release and sequestration has helped stabilize Earth's climate, making it possible for life to persist and evolve.

The Unique Nature of Earth's Tectonics and Life's Evolution

When we consider the potential for life elsewhere in the universe, one question arises: is plate tectonics a prerequisite for life? If Earth's plate tectonics have been essential to regulating its climate and providing the necessary conditions for life to emerge, could life also evolve on planets without tectonic activity? Scientists are beginning to explore this question as they study other planets in our solar system and beyond. Mars and Venus, for example, show signs of past tectonic activity but have since become geologically stagnant. Both planets are also inhospitable to life as we know it, raising the possibility that Earth's long-lasting tectonic processes have been uniquely conducive to life's development.

The Tectonics-Life Feedback Loop

Life and tectonics may not only be interconnected but may also form a feedback loop. Life itself, particularly microbial life, has played a role in shaping Earth's geology. For example, early photosynthetic organisms contributed to the oxygenation of Earth's atmosphere, which in turn influenced the chemical weathering of rocks. Similarly, plants have contributed to the erosion of mountains and the creation of soils. This interplay between life and Earth's tectonic activity suggests that, once life emerged, it became an active participant in the ongoing geological processes that continue to shape the planet.

Unraveling Earth's Deepest Mystery

The question of whether plate tectonics gave rise to life touches on some of the deepest mysteries of our planet's history. By exploring the connections between geology and biology, we can begin to understand how the Earth's dynamic processes created an environment where life could not only begin but also thrive and evolve. This book will take you on a journey through time, from the formation of the first tectonic plates to the appearance of

Did Plate Tectonics Give Rise to Life?

the earliest life forms, and beyond, into the ongoing relationship between Earth's deep geological forces and the life that inhabits its surface.

Through a careful examination of scientific evidence, we will explore how plate tectonics has shaped Earth's climate, oceans, and atmosphere in ways that may have been critical to life's emergence. Could Earth's unique tectonic processes be the key to understanding how life began? This is the mystery we will unravel as we delve deep into the science of Earth's geology and the origins of life.

Chapter 1: The Dynamic Earth – Understanding Plate Tectonics

The Earth, often described as a living planet, constantly reshapes itself through forces that operate deep beneath the surface. Among these, the theory of plate tectonics is perhaps the most fundamental in explaining the Earth's dynamic nature. Plate tectonics refers to the movement of large plates that make up Earth's outer shell, and it is responsible for shaping continents, forming mountains, triggering earthquakes, and fueling volcanic activity. This chapter introduces the concept of plate tectonics, its history, and the major processes that drive it.

The Origins of Plate Tectonic Theory

Plate tectonics is the result of centuries of scientific exploration and discovery. The first inklings of this theory can be traced back to the early 20th century when a German meteorologist and geophysicist named **Alfred Wegener** proposed the idea of **continental drift**. Wegener suggested that Earth's continents were once part of a supercontinent called **Pangaea**, which began to break apart around 200 million years ago. According to his theory, the pieces of Pangaea gradually drifted across the Earth's surface to form the continents we see today.

Wegener's theory was initially dismissed by much of the scientific community, largely because he couldn't explain the mechanism that drove the continents apart. However, his observations of how continents seemed to fit together like a jigsaw puzzle, and the discovery of similar fossilized plants and animals on continents now separated by oceans, were hard to ignore.

It wasn't until the 1960s, with the advent of new technologies like seafloor mapping and the discovery of **seafloor spreading**, that the scientific community fully embraced Wegener's ideas in a new form: plate tectonics. The theory was significantly bolstered by evidence from **paleomagnetism**, the study of Earth's magnetic field preserved in rocks. Patterns of magnetic stripes on the ocean floor provided proof that new crust was forming at **mid-ocean ridges** and spreading outward, pushing tectonic plates apart. This realization marked a paradigm shift in geology.

The Lithospheric Plates: Earth's Rigid Shell

Earth's outer shell, or **lithosphere**, is not a single, continuous layer. Instead, it is divided into numerous rigid pieces known as **tectonic plates**. These plates are composed of **continental crust** and **oceanic crust**, along with the rigid upper part of the mantle. Tectonic plates vary in size; some are vast and span entire oceans, such as the **Pacific Plate**, while others, like the **Nazca Plate**, are smaller but still play crucial roles in shaping Earth's geology.

The lithosphere floats atop the **asthenosphere**, a more ductile, semi-molten layer of the upper mantle. While the asthenosphere can flow and deform over long periods, the lithosphere remains brittle and rigid, which is why it cracks and shifts rather than bending smoothly.

There are seven major tectonic plates: the **Pacific**, **North American**, **South American**, **Eurasian**, **African**, **Indo-Australian**, and **Antarctic** plates. These plates are constantly in motion, albeit at a rate that is often imperceptible on a human timescale, typically moving at rates of a few centimeters per year—about the same speed at which fingernails grow. Nevertheless, over millions of years, these movements are responsible for dramatic shifts in Earth's surface.

Plate Boundaries: Where the Action Happens

The boundaries where tectonic plates interact are where most of Earth's seismic and volcanic activity occurs. Plate boundaries are classified into three main types based on the nature of their interactions: **divergent**, **convergent**, and **transform** boundaries.

1. **Divergent Boundaries**: At **divergent boundaries**, tectonic plates move away from each other. This type of boundary is most commonly found along **mid-ocean ridges**, such as the **Mid-Atlantic Ridge**, where new oceanic crust is formed as magma rises from the mantle to fill the gap between the plates. This process, known as **seafloor spreading**, continuously adds new material to the ocean floor, pushing older crust further away from the ridge. As the plates diverge, the lithosphere becomes thin, and magma from the mantle wells up to fill the void. This magma cools and solidifies to form new oceanic crust. Over millions of years, this process can create vast ocean basins, explaining how the Atlantic Ocean formed as the Americas drifted away from Europe and Africa.

2. **Convergent Boundaries**: In contrast to divergent boundaries, **convergent boundaries** occur where two plates move toward each other. This type of interaction can lead to some of the most dramatic geological events on Earth. There are three types of convergent boundaries based on the nature of the colliding plates:

   - **Oceanic-Continental Convergence**: When an oceanic plate collides with a continental plate, the denser oceanic crust is forced beneath the lighter continental crust in a process called **subduction**. As the oceanic plate sinks into the mantle, it melts, generating magma that can rise to form volcanic mountain ranges, such as the **Andes** in South America.

- **Oceanic-Oceanic Convergence**: When two oceanic plates collide, one is typically subducted beneath the other, forming **island arcs**—chains of volcanic islands like those found in the western Pacific, including Japan and the Philippines.
- **Continental-Continental Convergence**: When two continental plates collide, neither plate is easily subducted because both are composed of relatively buoyant crust. Instead, the plates crumple and fold, creating vast mountain ranges like the **Himalayas**, which formed from the collision of the Indian Plate with the Eurasian Plate.

3. **Transform Boundaries**: At **transform boundaries**, plates slide past one another horizontally. Unlike the other two types of boundaries, transform boundaries do not involve the creation or destruction of lithosphere. However, they are associated with intense seismic activity because the friction between the sliding plates often leads to the buildup of stress. When this stress is released, it causes earthquakes.

The most famous example of a transform boundary is the **San Andreas Fault** in California, where the Pacific Plate slides past the North American Plate.

Geological Features Created by Plate Tectonics

The movement of tectonic plates is responsible for creating many of Earth's most striking geological features. From towering mountains to deep ocean trenches, these features are the result of millions of years of tectonic activity.

- **Mountain Ranges**: The formation of mountains is perhaps the most visible effect of plate tectonics. **Orogeny**, the process of mountain building, occurs primarily at convergent boundaries, where plates collide. The **Himalayas**, the world's highest mountain range, are still rising today as the Indian Plate continues to push into the Eurasian Plate. Similarly, the **Rocky Mountains** in North America were formed through complex interactions at convergent plate boundaries.
- **Volcanoes**: Most of the Earth's volcanic activity is linked to tectonic plate movements. **Subduction zones** are prime locations for volcanic activity, where the subducting plate melts and creates magma that rises to the surface. This results in volcanic arcs, such as the **Ring of Fire** encircling the Pacific Ocean. In addition to subduction zones, **hotspots**,

areas of volcanic activity far from plate boundaries, also produce volcanoes, such as those forming the Hawaiian Islands.

- **Earthquakes**: Earthquakes are another byproduct of tectonic activity, particularly along **transform boundaries** and **subduction zones**. When plates grind against each other or get stuck, immense pressure builds up. Once this pressure is released, it causes seismic waves that shake the Earth's surface. Some of the most powerful earthquakes ever recorded have occurred along tectonic plate boundaries, including the 2011 **Tohoku earthquake** off the coast of Japan.

- **Ocean Basins and Trenches**: The **Atlantic and Pacific Oceans** owe their existence to plate tectonics. Ocean basins are formed by the divergence of plates at mid-ocean ridges. As new crust is created, the oceans widen, and deep **ocean trenches** are formed where plates converge. For example, the **Mariana Trench**, the deepest part of the world's oceans, was formed by the subduction of the Pacific Plate beneath the smaller Mariana Plate.

Modern Tools for Studying Plate Tectonics

Our understanding of plate tectonics has advanced dramatically thanks to modern technology. **GPS (Global Positioning System)** allows scientists to measure the movement of tectonic plates with incredible precision, often down to millimeters per year. This technology has provided real-time evidence of how continents shift and how plates interact at their boundaries.

Other tools, such as **seismometers**, help geologists detect and study earthquakes, offering insights into the behavior of tectonic plates during seismic events. **Satellite imaging** and **remote sensing** have also revolutionized our ability to study Earth's surface, revealing patterns of crustal deformation and volcanic activity linked to tectonics.

Conclusion

Plate tectonics is the engine that drives many of Earth's most dynamic processes. From the slow drift of continents to the violent shaking of earthquakes and the explosive power of volcanoes, the movement of tectonic plates shapes the world we live in. Understanding plate tectonics is essential not only for grasping the Earth's past but also for predicting future geological events and their impact on human life. In the chapters that follow, we will delve deeper into the connections between plate tectonics and the origins of life, uncovering how the planet's restless nature may have created the conditions necessary for life to begin.

Chapter 2: The Birth of Continents and Oceans

The Earth's continents and oceans are dynamic, ever-changing features that have evolved over billions of years due to the movement of tectonic plates. The theory of plate tectonics not only provides a comprehensive explanation for the current configuration of continents and oceans but also sheds light on how they have changed through time. This chapter delves into the processes responsible for the birth of continents and oceans, examining how the tectonic forces drive the formation of landmasses and ocean basins. We'll explore supercontinents such as Pangaea and Rodinia, the role of mid-ocean ridges, and the recycling of Earth's crust through subduction zones.

The Formation of Continents: A Tectonic Puzzle

When Earth formed around 4.5 billion years ago, it was a molten mass of rock and metal, with no solid surface. As the planet began to cool, a thin crust formed on its surface, giving rise to the first continents. These early landmasses were small and unstable, but over time, the process of plate tectonics created larger, more stable continents. Tectonic plates—the massive slabs of Earth's lithosphere—move slowly across the planet's surface, driven by heat from the planet's interior. As these plates collide, separate, or slide past one another, they shape the continents and oceans in an ongoing process that has occurred for billions of years.

Early Earth and the Crustal Formation

The earliest evidence of continental crust dates back to about 4.0 billion years ago. Initially, the Earth's surface was dominated by volcanic activity, which released molten rock from the mantle to form the earliest rocks. Over time, these rocks were recycled through various tectonic processes, and eventually, larger landmasses began to form. The gradual cooling of the Earth's mantle allowed for the differentiation between oceanic and continental crust.

The continental crust is relatively light and buoyant, composed mainly of granitic rocks. In contrast, the oceanic crust is denser and primarily composed of basalt. This difference in density plays a crucial role in the dynamics of plate tectonics, particularly in subduction zones, where denser oceanic plates are forced beneath the lighter continental plates.

Supercontinent Cycles: Pangaea and Rodinia

Throughout Earth's history, the continents have not remained in fixed positions. Instead, they have drifted across the planet's surface, occasionally colliding to form massive supercontinents. This cycle of continental aggregation and dispersal is known as the **supercontinent cycle**. It has repeated itself several times over Earth's 4.5 billion-year history, and each supercontinent has profoundly impacted the planet's geology, climate, and even the evolution of life.

Rodinia: An Early Supercontinent

One of the earliest known supercontinents is **Rodinia**, which formed around 1.1 billion years ago during the Proterozoic Eon. Rodinia was the result of several ancient land masses coming together, and it likely spanned much of the planet. Although little is known about its exact configuration, scientists believe that Rodinia's formation and breakup were pivotal in shaping Earth's early tectonic landscape.

The breakup of Rodinia, which occurred around 750 million years ago, may have triggered a series of dramatic geological and climatic events. One theory suggests that the breakup of Rodinia contributed to the onset of a global glaciation event known as **Snowball Earth**, during which the planet was covered in ice from pole to pole. This extreme climate may have played a crucial role in the evolution of early life by creating new ecological niches and driving biological innovation.

Pangaea: The Most Famous Supercontinent

The most well-known supercontinent, **Pangaea**, formed much later, around 335 million years ago during the late Paleozoic Era. Pangaea was a massive landmass that included nearly all of Earth's continents, stretching from the northern to the southern hemisphere. Its formation was the result of tectonic collisions between smaller landmasses, including Laurasia (North America, Europe, and parts of Asia) and Gondwana (Africa, South America, Australia, Antarctica, and the Indian subcontinent).

Pangaea's formation and eventual breakup had profound effects on Earth's climate and ecosystems. The supercontinent's interior was likely arid and desert-like, as it was far from the moderating influence of the oceans. Meanwhile, the breakup of Pangaea, which began around 175 million years ago during the Jurassic Period, reshaped Earth's oceans and created new coastlines, leading to changes in ocean circulation patterns and the distribution of life.

Mid-Ocean Ridges: The Birthplaces of New Crust

While the formation of supercontinents like Pangaea and Rodinia is a spectacular result of plate tectonics, the process that drives the movement of tectonic plates is equally fascinating. One of the most important tectonic features on Earth is the **mid-ocean ridge system**, where new oceanic crust is continuously formed.

Mid-ocean ridges are underwater mountain ranges that stretch across the ocean floor, marking the boundaries between tectonic plates. At these ridges, magma from Earth's mantle rises to the surface, creating new oceanic crust as the tectonic plates pull apart. This process, known as **seafloor spreading**, plays a central role in plate tectonics, as it drives the movement of plates across the Earth's surface.

The Role of Seafloor Spreading

As new oceanic crust forms at mid-ocean ridges, it gradually pushes the older crust away from the ridge, creating vast ocean basins. This process is responsible for the expansion of the Atlantic Ocean, as the Eurasian and North American plates pull apart along the Mid-Atlantic Ridge. Seafloor spreading also explains why the oldest oceanic crust is relatively young—no more than 200 million years old—compared to the ancient continental crust, which can be over 4 billion years old.

In addition to creating new crust, mid-ocean ridges are also home to some of Earth's most extreme environments, including hydrothermal vent systems. These vents, located along the ridges, support unique ecosystems that thrive in the absence of sunlight, relying instead on chemical energy from the Earth's interior. These environments may offer clues to the origin of life on Earth and the potential for life on other planets.

Subduction Zones: Recycling the Earth's Crust

While new crust is continuously created at mid-ocean ridges, old crust is recycled back into the Earth's mantle at **subduction zones**. Subduction occurs when one tectonic plate is forced beneath another, typically when a denser oceanic plate converges with a lighter continental plate. As the oceanic plate descends into the mantle, it melts, and the material is reabsorbed into the Earth's interior.

The Importance of Subduction in the Rock Cycle

Subduction is a critical part of the **rock cycle**, which describes the continuous recycling of Earth's crust. It plays a vital role in balancing the creation of new crust at mid-ocean ridges with the destruction of old crust at subduction zones. Without subduction, Earth's surface would be continuously expanding, and the planet's surface features would look very different.

Subduction zones are also the sites of some of Earth's most powerful geological phenomena, including **earthquakes** and **volcanic eruptions**. As the descending plate melts, it creates magma that rises to the surface, fueling volcanic activity. Some of the world's most active volcanic regions, such as the **Pacific Ring of Fire**, are located along subduction zones.

Subduction not only recycles crustal material but also contributes to the formation of mountain ranges. For example, the **Andes Mountains** in South America were formed by the subduction of the oceanic Nazca Plate beneath the continental South American Plate. Over millions of years, the immense forces generated by subduction can uplift and fold the Earth's crust, creating towering mountain ranges that reshape the landscape.

The Continuous Dance of Continents and Oceans

The birth of continents and oceans is not a singular event in Earth's history but an ongoing process that has shaped the planet for billions of years. The movement of tectonic plates, driven by forces deep within the Earth, continually reshapes the surface, creating new continents, ocean basins, and mountain ranges while recycling old crust back into the mantle.

The supercontinent cycles, the formation of new oceanic crust at mid-ocean ridges, and the recycling of crust at subduction zones are all part of the intricate dance of plate tectonics. This dynamic system has created the world we know today and will continue to shape the Earth's surface in the future, affecting everything from climate to the distribution of life.

As we look back at Earth's geological history, we gain a deeper appreciation for the forces that have shaped our planet and created the conditions necessary for life to thrive. Understanding the birth of continents and oceans not only helps us comprehend the past but also provides insights into the future of our ever-changing world.

Chapter 3: Earth's Early Atmosphere and Oceans – The Cradle of Life

The early Earth was a vastly different place from the planet we inhabit today. Instead of blue skies, vast oceans, and lush landscapes, it was a world dominated by violent volcanic activity, a chaotic atmosphere, and a molten surface. The conditions of this early Earth, about 4.5 billion years ago, were inhospitable to life as we know it. Yet, it is within this chaotic environment that the foundation for life was laid, with the atmosphere and oceans playing a crucial role. This chapter explores the processes that gave rise to Earth's early atmosphere and oceans, focusing on how volcanic outgassing and tectonic activity helped create a habitable environment—ultimately leading to the emergence of life.

Volcanic Outgassing: Shaping the Early Atmosphere

In Earth's infancy, its surface was a molten sea of magma, and as the planet began to cool, solid rock started to form. However, this cooling process did not happen quietly. Early Earth was marked by intense volcanic activity, with massive eruptions releasing vast amounts of gases from the interior of the planet into the developing atmosphere. This process, known as volcanic outgassing, was a critical mechanism in forming Earth's early atmosphere.

The Gases Released

The primary gasses released by volcanic activity included **water vapor (H_2O), carbon dioxide (CO_2), nitrogen (N_2), methane (CH_4), ammonia (NH_3)**, and trace amounts of other gasses such as **hydrogen (H_2)** and **sulfur dioxide (SO_2)**. The Earth's first atmosphere, referred to as the *primordial atmosphere*, was vastly different from what we breathe today. It lacked free oxygen (O_2) and was instead dominated by water vapor and carbon dioxide, along with other greenhouse gasses.

The Role of Water Vapor

The outgassing of water vapor was particularly significant. As the Earth continued to cool, much of this water vapor began to condense and fall as rain, contributing to the formation of the Earth's first oceans. It is estimated that volcanic outgassing over millions of years provided the vast majority of water that eventually filled the oceans. The presence of abundant water was essential, as it would later become a key solvent in the chemical processes that led to the origin of life.

Carbon Dioxide and the Greenhouse Effect

Carbon dioxide, another major component of volcanic outgassing, played a crucial role in regulating Earth's temperature. Despite the Sun being about 30% less luminous than it is today, Earth did not freeze over. This is because the thick early atmosphere, rich in CO_2, created a powerful greenhouse effect that trapped heat, maintaining relatively warm surface temperatures. Without this warming effect, Earth might have remained a frozen world, inhospitable to the chemical reactions necessary for life.

Nitrogen's Dominance

Nitrogen, which is a major component of our modern atmosphere, also began accumulating during this period. Although it did not participate in significant chemical reactions, its presence contributed to the atmosphere's overall composition. Over time, nitrogen became the dominant gas in Earth's atmosphere, providing a stable backdrop against which other gases and compounds interacted.

Ocean Formation: The Role of Tectonics in Earth's Hydrological Cycle

Did Plate Tectonics Give Rise to Life? As water vapor condensed and fell to the Earth's surface, it began filling the planet's low-lying areas, giving rise to the first oceans. This was a crucial step in Earth's development, as oceans would later become the cradle of life. But the formation and stability of Earth's oceans were not solely the result of cooling; tectonic processes played a vital role in shaping the hydrological cycle and maintaining the oceans over geological time scales.

The Early Ocean Basin

Tectonic activity is responsible for creating the basins that hold Earth's oceans. As the Earth's lithosphere cooled, it fractured into tectonic plates, which began to move. The movement of these plates created depressions in the Earth's surface, where water could accumulate. Mid-ocean ridges, where new oceanic crust is formed through seafloor spreading, and subduction zones, where oceanic crust is pushed into the mantle, were crucial in defining the geography of Earth's oceans.

Continental Formation and Ocean Stabilization

The tectonic movements also contributed to the formation of early continental landmasses. As lighter materials, such as silica, rose to the surface, large continental plates formed. The interaction between oceanic and continental plates played a significant role in stabilizing the planet's water cycle. Volcanic islands and continents acted as barriers, preventing the oceans from evaporating too quickly or dissipating into space.

Water Cycle Regulation by Tectonic Activity

Tectonic activity continues to regulate Earth's water cycle through processes like subduction, where oceanic plates are forced beneath continental plates. This process drives water deep into the Earth's mantle, where it can be stored and later released through volcanic activity. This cycle of water moving between the surface and the interior of the planet ensures that Earth's oceans have remained relatively stable over billions of years.

The long-term stability of Earth's oceans provided a stable environment for chemical processes that led to life. In particular, the ocean acted as a vast chemical reactor, allowing early organic molecules to interact and form more complex compounds, setting the stage for the development of life.

Atmospheric Changes: The Evolution of Earth's Early Atmosphere

As volcanic outgassing continued, the composition of Earth's atmosphere evolved. Initially, the atmosphere was reducing, meaning it lacked free oxygen. However, this environment was conducive to the formation of simple organic molecules, which would later be crucial in the development of life. Over time, the interactions between Earth's atmosphere, oceans, and tectonic processes led to significant changes in the atmospheric composition.

The Role of Tectonics in Atmospheric Evolution

Tectonic activity had a profound impact on the evolution of Earth's atmosphere. The movement of tectonic plates influenced volcanic eruptions, which in turn affected the atmospheric composition. For example, subduction-related volcanic activity released large amounts of gases like carbon dioxide and water vapor, which contributed to the greenhouse effect and maintained Earth's surface temperature. Tectonic processes also played a role in the cycling of elements between the Earth's surface and interior, influencing the availability of key compounds like carbon and sulfur.

The Great Oxygenation Event

One of the most significant changes in Earth's atmosphere occurred around 2.4 billion years ago, during the Great Oxygenation Event (GOE). Before this event, Earth's atmosphere contained very little free oxygen. However, the emergence of cyanobacteria, which used photosynthesis to convert carbon dioxide and water into oxygen and glucose, gradually increased oxygen levels in the atmosphere. This biological change was directly tied to tectonic activity, as plate movements influenced the distribution of landmasses and ocean basins, which in turn affected the spread of photosynthetic organisms.

The Impact on Life

The rise of oxygen in Earth's atmosphere was both a blessing and a curse for early life forms. While oxygen allowed for the development of more complex, energy-efficient life forms, it was toxic to many of the anaerobic organisms that had thrived in the reducing atmosphere. This shift in atmospheric composition led to one of Earth's first mass extinctions but also paved the way for the evolution of aerobic organisms, which would eventually dominate the planet.

Conclusion: Tectonics, Atmosphere, and the Emergence of Life

The early Earth's atmosphere and oceans were not static; they were shaped by dynamic geological processes, particularly volcanic outgassing and tectonic activity. These processes not only created the physical environment necessary for life but also influenced the chemical composition of the atmosphere and oceans, making them suitable for the complex interactions that would eventually lead to the origin of life.

Volcanic outgassing provided the essential gases, including water vapor and carbon dioxide, that formed the early atmosphere and oceans. Meanwhile, tectonic processes played a key role in shaping the geography of the planet, stabilizing the hydrological cycle, and regulating the Earth's climate over billions of years. The interaction between these geological processes and the atmosphere set the stage for the emergence of life, demonstrating that Earth's geological and biological histories are deeply intertwined.

In the chapters that follow, we will explore how these early conditions, driven by plate tectonics, continued to evolve, setting the stage for the emergence and diversification of life on Earth.

Chapter 4: Hydrothermal Vents – The Possible Cradle of Life

The question of how life originated on Earth is one of the greatest mysteries in science. Among the many hypotheses that have been proposed, one of the most fascinating involves the deep ocean hydrothermal vents, which form in environments where tectonic plates are actively moving apart. These underwater fissures, often located along mid-ocean ridges, release superheated, mineral-rich water into the surrounding ocean, creating extreme conditions that are vastly different from the sunlit surface of the Earth.

Hydrothermal vents present a unique, energy-rich environment, and some scientists believe they may have been the cradle of life on Earth. This chapter delves into the characteristics of these vents, the types of ecosystems they support, and the theories that suggest they could have played a critical role in the emergence of life. By exploring the interaction of geology, chemistry, and biology at these deep-sea sites, we can gain insights into the potential pathways that might have led to the first life forms on Earth.

1. Black Smokers and White Smokers: The Dynamic Vent Systems

Hydrothermal vents are found in regions of the ocean where tectonic plates are diverging, such as along mid-ocean ridges, where magma from the Earth's mantle rises to create new oceanic crust. The most common types of hydrothermal vents are known as **black smokers** and **white smokers**, named for the appearance of the plumes they emit into the water.

- **Black Smokers**: These vents release superheated water, often exceeding temperatures of 350°C (662°F), that is rich in dissolved metals like iron and sulfur. When this hot water encounters the near-freezing temperatures of the deep ocean, the dissolved metals precipitate out, forming black clouds of metal sulfides—hence the name. The chimneys around black smokers are built up from these metal deposits and can reach impressive heights, sometimes towering more than 60 meters (200 feet) above the seafloor.
- **White Smokers**: In contrast, white smokers emit cooler water, typically around 200-300°C (392-572°F), and their plumes are lighter in color due to the different minerals they contain, such as barium, calcium, and silicon. These minerals give the vent plumes a white or pale appearance. White smokers

tend to form at different depths compared to black smokers and may host different communities of organisms.

Both types of smokers are located along mid-ocean ridges, where tectonic activity creates the conditions for seawater to percolate through cracks in the Earth's crust. As this water is heated by magma beneath the seafloor, it dissolves minerals from the surrounding rocks, which are then expelled through the vent openings, creating a mineral-rich environment.

2. Chemical Energy: Life Thriving Without Sunlight

One of the most remarkable discoveries about hydrothermal vents is that they support entire ecosystems in the absence of sunlight. Most life on Earth relies on photosynthesis, the process by which plants and other organisms convert sunlight into energy. However, in the deep ocean, sunlight cannot penetrate, leaving these regions in permanent darkness. Despite this, life flourishes around hydrothermal vents, and the key to their survival is a process known as **chemosynthesis**.

- **Chemosynthesis**: Instead of relying on sunlight for energy, organisms around hydrothermal vents harness chemical energy from the compounds released by the vents. At the heart of this process is the conversion of chemicals like hydrogen sulfide (H_2S) and methane (CH_4) into organic matter. In particular, bacteria and archaea living near the vents use these chemicals as energy sources to fix carbon and produce the organic compounds that form the basis of the vent ecosystem.

These microorganisms form the foundation of the food web in vent ecosystems, much like plants do in surface ecosystems. Larger organisms, such as tubeworms, clams, and shrimp, either directly consume these microbes or have symbiotic relationships with them. For example, giant tubeworms (Riftia pachyptila) that live near black smokers have no digestive system of their own; instead, they host chemosynthetic bacteria inside their bodies, which produce food for both the bacteria and the tubeworm.

This ability to harness energy from chemicals rather than sunlight is a crucial aspect of the hypothesis that hydrothermal vents could have been the birthplace of life on Earth. Early Earth lacked oxygen in its atmosphere, and life may have emerged in environments where chemical energy was abundant, such as hydrothermal vents.

3. Origin of Life Hypotheses: The Role of Vents in Life's Emergence

The idea that life may have originated around hydrothermal vents is supported by several key factors, including the abundance of chemical energy, the presence of essential minerals, and the unique conditions that could have fostered the synthesis of the first life-sustaining molecules.

- **Prebiotic Chemistry**: One of the central challenges in origin-of-life research is understanding how simple molecules, such as amino acids and nucleotides, could have combined to form the more complex structures required for life, like proteins and RNA. Hydrothermal vents provide a potential solution to this problem. The mineral-rich fluids expelled by the vents contain essential elements like sulfur, iron, and magnesium, which could have acted as catalysts for prebiotic chemical reactions. These reactions might have produced the building blocks of life, such as amino acids and fatty acids, under high-pressure, high-temperature conditions similar to those found at hydrothermal vents.

- **The Role of Minerals**: Certain minerals found in vent environments, particularly those containing iron and sulfur, may have played a role in the early chemistry of life. For example, iron-sulfur clusters are essential components of many enzymes in modern cells, suggesting that these minerals could have been involved in the earliest metabolic processes. Additionally, clay minerals found around hydrothermal vents may have provided surfaces where organic molecules could assemble and interact, increasing the chances of forming complex compounds.

- **The Alkaline Vent Hypothesis**: A specific type of hydrothermal vent, known as an **alkaline hydrothermal vent**, has garnered particular attention in origin-of-life research. These vents, unlike black smokers, release water that is rich in hydrogen and has a higher pH (more alkaline). The contrast between the acidic ocean water and the alkaline vent fluids could have created natural proton gradients, which are a fundamental feature of modern cellular metabolism. In modern cells, proton gradients across membranes power the production of ATP, the energy currency of life. Some scientists hypothesize that similar gradients at alkaline vents could have driven the first biochemical reactions that led to the emergence of life.

- **Compartments and Early Cells**: Another important factor in the origin of life is the need for compartmentalization—keeping reactive chemicals together while excluding others. The porous, chimney-like structures formed by hydrothermal vents could have provided natural compartments where prebiotic chemistry could take place. These mineral "cells" might have acted as precursors to the lipid-based membranes found in modern cells, creating enclosed environments where complex chemical reactions could occur.

---

4. Hydrothermal Vents as Potential Sites for the Origin of Life

The deep-sea hydrothermal vent hypothesis for the origin of life offers several advantages over the traditional "primordial soup" model, which suggests that life began in shallow ponds or oceans through a series of random chemical reactions.

- **Stable Environment**: Hydrothermal vents offer a relatively stable environment compared to surface conditions, which would have been subject to extreme fluctuations in temperature, radiation from the sun, and meteor impacts during Earth's early history. The consistent supply of chemical energy and the protection from harmful ultraviolet (UV) radiation provided by the deep ocean make hydrothermal vents an appealing candidate for the birthplace of life.
- **Energy Availability**: The continuous flow of energy from the Earth's interior, in the form of heat and chemicals like hydrogen sulfide, provided a constant

energy source for early life. This energy flow is critical, as all living organisms require a consistent energy supply to drive metabolic processes and maintain complexity.

- **Extremophiles**: Modern organisms that thrive in extreme environments, known as extremophiles, provide clues to what early life on Earth might have been like. Many extremophiles, particularly thermophiles (heat-loving organisms) and chemolithoautotrophs (organisms that derive energy from inorganic compounds), are found around hydrothermal vents. These organisms are considered living fossils, possibly resembling some of the earliest life forms on Earth.

Conclusion: Hydrothermal Vents – The Birthplace of Life?

While no definitive proof yet exists that life began at hydrothermal vents, the unique conditions present at these sites make them a compelling candidate. The combination of chemical energy, essential minerals, and natural compartments could have provided the ideal environment for the synthesis of life's first molecules. Whether or not life began in the deep sea, the discovery of thriving ecosystems around hydrothermal vents has expanded our understanding of the diversity and resilience of life, offering a glimpse into how life could arise in the most unexpected places—on Earth or even on other planets with similar conditions.

Chapter 5: Plate Tectonics and Earth's Climate – A Delicate Balance

Plate tectonics is not just a geological process that moves continents and builds mountains; it plays a critical role in shaping the Earth's climate system. This dynamic process, which shifts the Earth's crustal plates over millions of years, has a profound influence on long-term climate patterns. The interactions between tectonic movements, ocean circulation, atmospheric chemistry, and the carbon cycle are complex and interconnected. Through these interactions, plate tectonics helps regulate the Earth's climate, making it stable enough for life to develop, evolve, and thrive.

This chapter explores the key ways plate tectonics has influenced Earth's climate, focusing on three major concepts: the carbon cycle, ice ages and warm periods, and mountain building. These processes illustrate how the slow and powerful movements of the Earth's plates create feedback mechanisms that maintain a delicate balance in the planet's climate over geological timescales.

The Carbon Cycle: Earth's Thermostat

The carbon cycle is central to regulating the Earth's climate. Carbon dioxide (CO_2), a greenhouse gas, traps heat in the Earth's atmosphere, which makes it one of the most important drivers of climate. Plate tectonics plays a fundamental role in controlling CO_2 levels through processes like subduction, volcanic eruptions, and weathering. These mechanisms create a long-term carbon feedback system that helps to keep Earth's climate within a range that supports life.

Subduction and Volcanism: The Carbon Release and Storage Mechanism

One of the most critical tectonic processes that regulate CO_2 is subduction. At convergent plate boundaries, oceanic plates, which contain large amounts of carbon, are forced beneath continental plates in a process known as subduction. As these plates descend into the Earth's mantle, carbonates from marine sediments are carried deep underground. Over time, this carbon can be stored in the mantle for millions of years, effectively removing CO_2 from the surface environment and reducing atmospheric concentrations.

However, tectonics also plays a role in releasing CO_2 back into the atmosphere. Volcanic activity, which often occurs at plate boundaries, is a significant source of atmospheric

CO_2. As subducted plates melt and form magma, some of the carbon stored in the Earth's mantle is released back into the atmosphere during volcanic eruptions. This release of CO_2 through volcanism contributes to maintaining a balance between carbon storage and emission, allowing Earth's climate to remain relatively stable over geological timescales.

Weathering and Carbon Sequestration: A Tectonic Cooling Mechanism

Another essential component of the carbon cycle regulated by plate tectonics is the process of silicate weathering, which serves as a natural carbon sequestration mechanism. When mountains are uplifted by tectonic forces, rocks are exposed to the atmosphere and subjected to weathering. During chemical weathering, carbon dioxide from the atmosphere reacts with silicate minerals in rocks to form bicarbonate ions, which are carried to the oceans by rivers. In the ocean, these ions precipitate to form carbonate minerals, effectively removing CO_2 from the atmosphere and sequestering it in marine sediments.

This process is especially effective in reducing atmospheric CO_2 and cooling the planet over long periods. For instance, during times of increased mountain building, such as the formation of the Himalayas, enhanced weathering has been linked to significant reductions in atmospheric CO_2, contributing to cooler global temperatures. Over millions of years, this tectonic-driven weathering process acts as a planetary thermostat, helping to prevent runaway greenhouse or icehouse conditions.

Ice Ages and Warm Periods: The Role of Tectonics in Climate Shifts

Throughout Earth's history, there have been periods of dramatic climate change, including ice ages and warm periods, many of which were influenced by tectonic forces. The movement of continents can profoundly affect global climate by altering ocean circulation patterns, changing the distribution of land masses, and even influencing the planet's axial tilt. These factors contribute to the cyclical nature of Earth's climate, marked by alternating glaciations and interglacial warm periods.

Continental Drift and Ocean Currents: Controlling Earth's Climate Engine

One of the most significant ways that tectonics affects the Earth's climate is through the movement of continents, which alters ocean circulation patterns. Oceans play a crucial role in distributing heat across the planet by transporting warm water from the equator to the poles and cold water from the poles to the tropics. This heat exchange is essential in moderating global climate.

When continents move due to plate tectonics, ocean currents are forced to change their paths. For example, the opening of the Drake Passage between South America and Antarctica around 34 million years ago allowed the development of the Antarctic Circumpolar Current. This current isolated Antarctica from warm ocean waters, contributing to the cooling of the continent and the onset of the Antarctic Ice Sheet. Similarly, the closure of the Isthmus of Panama around 3 million years ago redirected ocean currents and strengthened the Gulf Stream, which helped warm northern Europe and may have contributed to the current ice age cycle.

Continental positioning also plays a role in climate by influencing the Earth's albedo (the reflectivity of the Earth's surface). Large landmasses near the poles can become glaciated, increasing the Earth's albedo and reflecting more solar energy back into space, leading to further cooling. Conversely, when continents are positioned closer to the equator, less glaciation occurs, reducing the planet's albedo and contributing to a warmer global climate.

Ice Age Cycles: The Intersection of Tectonics and Orbital Changes

Did Plate Tectonics Give Rise to Life?

Ice ages, or glacial periods, are times when large parts of the Earth's surface become covered by ice sheets. While variations in the Earth's orbit (known as Milankovitch cycles) are a major driver of these cycles, tectonics can amplify or diminish the effects of orbital changes. For example, the formation of high-altitude plateaus like the Tibetan Plateau due to tectonic uplift can create favorable conditions for glaciation by increasing the area where ice and snow accumulate. Additionally, tectonic-driven changes in the distribution of continents and ocean circulation can trigger feedback loops that either promote or reduce glacial periods.

Conversely, during periods of tectonic activity that lead to increased volcanic eruptions, higher levels of CO_2 can create a greenhouse effect, warming the planet and potentially ending glaciations. The balance between these competing forces – tectonics driving cooling via weathering and glaciation, and volcanism contributing to warming – illustrates the delicate interplay between tectonics and climate.

Mountain Building: Tectonic Influence on Weather Patterns and Erosion

The rise of mountain ranges due to plate tectonics not only affects local landscapes but also has far-reaching consequences for global climate. Mountain building, or orogeny, alters atmospheric circulation, enhances weathering processes, and affects precipitation patterns. These changes contribute to long-term climate shifts and play a key role in regulating the planet's temperature and atmospheric composition.

Mountains as Climate Modifiers: Rain Shadows and Atmospheric Circulation

As tectonic forces push continental plates together, they create towering mountain ranges like the Himalayas and the Andes. These mountains act as barriers to atmospheric circulation, altering wind and precipitation patterns. For example, the Himalayas block moist air from the Indian Ocean, creating a rain shadow effect that leads to the arid conditions of the Tibetan Plateau and Central Asia. On the windward side, however, these same mountains cause intense rainfall, influencing monsoon patterns and providing vital moisture to ecosystems and human populations.

Mountain ranges also affect global atmospheric circulation. The uplift of large landmasses can divert jet streams and alter the distribution of pressure systems, influencing weather patterns far beyond the immediate vicinity of the mountains. This tectonic influence on atmospheric circulation can lead to long-term changes in climate, particularly in regions that rely on predictable weather patterns for agriculture and water resources.

Enhanced Weathering and Erosion: Cooling the Planet

The formation of mountains through tectonic uplift also accelerates weathering and erosion, both of which are critical for regulating the Earth's climate. As mountains rise, they expose fresh rock to the atmosphere, where it undergoes chemical weathering. This process draws CO_2 from the atmosphere, sequestering it in the form of carbonates that are eventually deposited in ocean sediments. The enhanced weathering of mountain ranges, especially in tropical regions where chemical weathering is most effective, acts as a negative feedback mechanism, cooling the planet over millions of years.

In addition to weathering, mountains are subject to erosion, which transports sediments from high elevations to lowlands and oceans. This erosion further contributes to the carbon cycle by burying organic carbon in sediments, effectively locking it away from the atmosphere. The combination of weathering and erosion driven by tectonic uplift is a powerful force in maintaining the long-term balance of CO_2 in the atmosphere, preventing extreme shifts in climate.

Conclusion: The Interplay Between Tectonics and Climate

The relationship between plate tectonics and Earth's climate is a complex and intricate system of feedback and interactions. From regulating atmospheric CO_2 levels through volcanic activity and weathering to altering ocean currents and atmospheric circulation, tectonic processes play a central role in shaping the Earth's climate over geological timescales. By creating conditions that promote long-term stability, plate tectonics has been instrumental in making Earth a habitable planet.

Through the delicate balance of tectonic forces, life on Earth has been able to survive and thrive for billions of years. While tectonic activity can trigger dramatic shifts in climate, it also acts as a stabilizing force, preventing runaway climate scenarios that could make the planet inhospitable. Understanding this balance helps us appreciate the interconnectedness of Earth's systems and underscores the importance of tectonics in the grand story of life on Earth.

Chapter 6: Life Shapes the Planet, and the Planet Shapes Life

The story of Earth is one of continuous transformation, with dynamic interactions between geology and biology at its core. Plate tectonics, a driving force behind the reshaping of Earth's surface, has long been understood to play a crucial role in creating the conditions necessary for life. However, what is often overlooked is the reciprocal relationship between life and the planet's geological processes. Life, from the tiniest microbes to vast forests, has influenced Earth's geology just as much as the tectonic forces that shaped it. This chapter delves into this symbiotic relationship, highlighting how life and tectonics are part of a feedback loop that has evolved over billions of years, altering the Earth's surface, atmosphere, and the very processes that govern its geological behavior.

The Co-Evolution of Life and Earth's Systems

When we consider the Earth as a system, it becomes clear that the biological and geological components are inextricably linked. Plate tectonics, volcanism, and erosion provide the necessary environments and nutrients for life, while life, in turn, transforms the landscape, alters the atmosphere, and influences the climate. Over time, these interactions have driven evolutionary changes in organisms and reshaped the planet itself.

Life on Earth did not merely evolve in response to a static environment; instead, it has played an active role in transforming that environment. From the ancient cyanobacteria that helped oxygenate the atmosphere, to the forests and root systems that drive modern erosion and sedimentation processes, organisms have left their mark on the planet's geochemical cycles and physical landscape.

Biogeochemical Cycles: Life's Role in Elemental Cycling

At the heart of this life-geology interaction are biogeochemical cycles, the processes by which elements like carbon, nitrogen, and oxygen are exchanged between living organisms and the Earth's atmosphere, oceans, and crust. These cycles are fundamental to maintaining life on the planet, and their existence is profoundly influenced by tectonic activity.

1. The Carbon Cycle:

One of the most critical biogeochemical cycles is the carbon cycle, where carbon is exchanged between the atmosphere, biosphere, oceans, and lithosphere. Plate tectonics plays a significant role in regulating the long-term carbon cycle through volcanic outgassing and the subduction of carbon-rich oceanic plates into the mantle, where carbon can be sequestered for millions of years.

Life, however, plays a vital role in the short-term carbon cycle. Photosynthetic organisms, including plants, algae, and cyanobacteria, absorb carbon dioxide from the atmosphere and convert it into organic compounds through photosynthesis. When these organisms die, the carbon stored in their bodies can either be released back into the atmosphere through respiration and decomposition, or become buried in sediments, eventually forming fossil fuels. Over millions of years, tectonic forces may uplift these carbon-rich sediments, leading to the release of carbon through volcanic activity or the burning of fossil fuels, further connecting life with geological processes.

2. The Nitrogen Cycle:

Nitrogen, essential for all life forms, is another key element cycled through biological and geological systems. The nitrogen cycle relies heavily on microbial life, particularly bacteria that can "fix" nitrogen from the atmosphere into a form that plants and other organisms can use. These nitrogen-fixing bacteria live in soil, water, and symbiotic relationships with plants. Over time, tectonic processes such as mountain building can expose nitrogen-rich rocks, making this element more available for microbial processing and thereby influencing local ecosystems.

However, nitrogen also impacts geological processes. As plants grow, they extract nitrogen from the soil and, upon decay, return nitrogen to the soil, where it can become part of the sedimentary cycle. Plate tectonics, by creating mountains and eroding sediments, contributes to the long-term storage and recycling of nitrogen, demonstrating how closely biological and geological processes are linked.

3. The Oxygen Cycle:

The oxygen cycle is intimately tied to life, particularly through the process of photosynthesis. Billions of years ago, when the first photosynthetic organisms evolved, they began to release oxygen as a byproduct, which slowly accumulated in the atmosphere during the Great Oxygenation Event. This oxygenation of the atmosphere was a prerequisite for the evolution of complex aerobic life forms.

Tectonics also influences the oxygen cycle. Volcanic eruptions can release oxygen-consuming gases like sulfur dioxide into the atmosphere, impacting oxygen levels. Furthermore, the burial of organic carbon in sediments, facilitated by tectonic processes like subduction, helps maintain atmospheric oxygen levels by preventing the carbon from oxidizing and consuming free oxygen. Thus, the oxygen cycle is both driven by life and influenced by the movements of the Earth's crust.

Erosion and Sedimentation: Life's Role in Shaping the Landscape

Life does not merely influence the chemistry of Earth's systems; it also plays a critical role in shaping the physical landscape. One of the most direct ways life interacts with geological processes is through erosion and sedimentation. While tectonic forces build mountains and create new landforms, living organisms, particularly plants and microbes, contribute to the breakdown and transport of these geological structures.

1. Biological Weathering:

Plants, fungi, and microorganisms are powerful agents of weathering. Plant roots can penetrate cracks in rocks, gradually breaking them apart as the roots grow and expand. Microbes and lichens produce acids that chemically break down minerals, further contributing to the disintegration of rocks. Over time, these biological processes accelerate the erosion of mountains and the breakdown of exposed bedrock, turning solid rock into soil.

2. Soil Formation:

The role of life in creating soil is one of the most critical processes linking biology and geology. Soil forms from the weathering of rocks and the accumulation of organic matter from plants and animals. Plate tectonics, by creating mountain ranges and exposing new rocks, sets the stage for soil formation, but it is the presence of life—plants, bacteria, fungi—that turns rock into fertile soil. This soil, in turn, sustains more life, creating a cycle of biological and geological interdependence.

3. Sediment Transport:

Once eroded, sediments are transported by wind, water, and glaciers. However, life also plays an active role in this process. Rivers, which are home to many forms of aquatic life, carry sediment downstream, where it is deposited in deltas and floodplains. These sediments often contain organic material that contributes to the formation of coal and other fossil fuels. Tectonic uplift can later expose these sedimentary layers, continuing the cycle of erosion and deposition.

Biological Innovations: Life's Adaptation to Geological Changes

As life and tectonic processes have evolved together, life has continuously adapted to changes in the Earth's geology. Each shift in the planet's landscape, from the rising of mountain ranges to the opening of new oceans, has created new challenges and opportunities for organisms. In response, life has developed innovative strategies to survive and thrive in constantly changing environments.

1. Evolution of Terrestrial Life:

The emergence of land plants around 470 million years ago marked a major evolutionary milestone in Earth's history. As tectonic activity continued to uplift continents and expose vast areas of land, plants began to colonize these areas, fundamentally altering the planet's atmosphere and ecosystems. The ability of plants to photosynthesize and release oxygen transformed Earth's atmosphere, creating the conditions necessary for the evolution of more complex terrestrial life forms, including animals.

2. Formation of New Habitats:

Tectonic activity creates new habitats by forming mountain ranges, rift valleys, and islands. Organisms have evolved to exploit these new environments. For example, island ecosystems are often hotspots for biodiversity due to their isolation. The Galápagos Islands, formed by volcanic activity, provided the setting for Darwin's observations on natural selection, illustrating how geological processes can directly influence biological evolution.

Similarly, deep-sea hydrothermal vents, created by tectonic activity along mid-ocean ridges, host unique ecosystems that thrive in complete darkness, using chemical energy rather than sunlight. These vent communities are an example of life's ability to adapt to extreme environments created by tectonic processes.

3. Ice Ages and Climate Change:

Tectonic shifts can also drive long-term changes in Earth's climate, influencing the evolution of life. For example, the rise of the Himalayas altered global wind and ocean currents, contributing to the onset of the Ice Ages. Organisms that survived these glaciations developed new adaptations, such as the thick fur of woolly mammoths or the migration patterns of birds, demonstrating how life continues to evolve in response to the planet's geological changes.

Conclusion: A Feedback Loop of Life and Geology

The relationship between life and geology is a powerful feedback loop, with each continuously influencing the other. Tectonic processes create the environments and conditions necessary for life, while life, in turn, alters the Earth's surface, atmosphere, and climate. Through biogeochemical cycles, erosion, and biological innovations, life has reshaped the planet just as much as tectonics have shaped life's evolution. As we look to the future, understanding this intricate dance between biology and geology will be key to deciphering not only Earth's past but also the conditions that might support life on other planets.

Chapter 7: Mass Extinctions and Tectonic Upheavals

The history of life on Earth is punctuated by catastrophic events that have wiped out vast numbers of species in short geological periods, reshaping the course of evolution. These mass extinctions, while devastating to biodiversity, have also played a crucial role in the emergence of new life forms by creating opportunities for surviving species to adapt and thrive in altered environments. One of the most significant forces driving these mass extinctions is tectonic activity, which has triggered volcanic eruptions, climate changes, and the breakup of supercontinents. This chapter delves into the profound connections between tectonic upheavals and mass extinctions, focusing on two of the most dramatic extinction events in Earth's history: the Permian-Triassic Extinction (also known as the "Great Dying") and the Cretaceous-Paleogene (K-T) Boundary Event.

The Permian Extinction: Earth's Deadliest Mass Extinction

Approximately 252 million years ago, at the end of the Permian period, the Earth experienced the most catastrophic extinction event in its history, wiping out around 90-96% of all marine species and 70% of terrestrial vertebrate species. This event, known as the Permian-Triassic Extinction or "The Great Dying," marked a turning point for life on Earth. The causes of this mass extinction remain the subject of ongoing scientific debate, but tectonic activity and its associated consequences are believed to have played a central role.

Tectonic Triggers and the Siberian Traps

One of the leading hypotheses for the Permian extinction centers on the massive volcanic activity in what is now Siberia, where an enormous volcanic province known as the **Siberian Traps** erupted for hundreds of thousands of years. These eruptions were not just typical volcanoes but involved the outpouring of flood basalts—huge amounts of lava that covered vast regions of land. This prolonged volcanic activity was likely driven by tectonic processes, specifically the movement of Earth's plates, which caused magma to rise from deep within the mantle.

The eruption of the Siberian Traps had devastating effects on the planet's climate and ecosystems. The release of **carbon dioxide (CO2)**, **methane**, and **sulfur dioxide** into the atmosphere created a greenhouse effect, leading to **global warming**. At the same time, the release of sulfur aerosols likely triggered **acid rain** and **ocean acidification**, disrupting marine ecosystems. The warming of the planet reduced the amount of oxygen in the oceans, creating vast **anoxic zones**, or "dead zones," where most marine life could not survive. The combination of these factors—global warming, ocean acidification, and anoxia—wiped out nearly all marine species, including the dominant trilobites and many coral species.

Supercontinent Breakup and Climate Instability

In addition to volcanic activity, the tectonic movements during the Permian period were significant. During this time, the supercontinent **Pangaea** was in the process of forming, as almost all of Earth's landmasses had come together. This formation of a supercontinent drastically altered the global climate. Pangaea's massive size created extreme interior deserts, as regions far from the coast were deprived of moisture. The merging of landmasses also disrupted ocean currents and atmospheric circulation patterns, which further contributed to climate instability.

The collision of tectonic plates not only created mountains but also caused fluctuations in sea levels, which were particularly devastating for marine environments. Shallow coastal ecosystems were especially vulnerable to these changes, and many species were unable to adapt to the rapidly shifting conditions. The overall loss of habitat and dramatic climate changes are believed to have been key drivers in the extinction of both marine and terrestrial species.

The K-T Boundary Event: A Double Catastrophe

While the Permian-Triassic Extinction was the deadliest mass extinction, the **Cretaceous-Paleogene (K-T) Boundary Event**, which occurred about 66 million years ago, is perhaps the most famous. This event is best known for causing the extinction of the non-avian dinosaurs, along with 75% of all species on Earth, and it marked the end of the Mesozoic Era. The K-T extinction event is often associated with the impact of a large asteroid or comet, but tectonic processes also played a significant role in shaping the planet's environment and contributing to the devastation.

The Chicxulub Impact

The asteroid impact hypothesis was first proposed in 1980 when scientists discovered a layer of **iridium**, a rare element often found in meteorites, at the K-T boundary in geological records worldwide. This layer corresponds to a massive asteroid impact that struck the Yucatán Peninsula, creating the **Chicxulub Crater**, which measures about 150 kilometers (93 miles) in diameter.

The immediate effects of the impact were catastrophic. The energy released from the collision would have been equivalent to billions of atomic bombs, generating shockwaves, massive wildfires, and tsunamis. The debris thrown into the atmosphere likely blocked sunlight for months, causing a "nuclear winter" effect. This sudden drop in temperatures would have devastated ecosystems, particularly photosynthetic organisms at the base of the food chain. Without sunlight, plant life perished, leading to a collapse in herbivore populations, which in turn affected carnivores.

Volcanism and the Deccan Traps

While the Chicxulub impact was a major factor in the K-T extinction, it was not the only one. Around the same time, Earth was experiencing extensive volcanic activity in what is now India. The **Deccan Traps**, a large volcanic province, erupted over a period of hundreds of thousands of years, releasing enormous quantities of **lava**, **CO2**, and other gases into the atmosphere. Like the Siberian Traps, these eruptions would have contributed to global warming and ocean acidification, further stressing ecosystems already weakened by the asteroid impact.

The combination of the Chicxulub impact and Deccan Traps volcanism created a **double catastrophe** that overwhelmed Earth's biosphere. While the asteroid may have been the "final straw" for many species, the long-term effects of volcanic activity had likely already destabilized the planet's ecosystems. This one-two punch wiped out not only the dinosaurs but also many marine species, plants, and small organisms, fundamentally reshaping life on Earth.

Survival and Adaptation: Life After Extinction

Despite the immense destruction caused by mass extinctions, there have also been periods of **evolutionary opportunity**. In the aftermath of these events, new species have emerged, evolving to fill ecological niches left vacant by extinct organisms. This section explores how life rebounds after mass extinctions and the patterns of adaptation that follow.

The Rise of Mammals

One of the most remarkable examples of life adapting to a post-extinction world occurred after the K-T boundary event. With the extinction of the non-avian dinosaurs, many ecological niches were left unoccupied. This allowed **mammals**, which had been relatively small and marginalized during the age of dinosaurs, to diversify and evolve into a wide variety of forms. In the millions of years that followed, mammals spread across the planet, giving rise to many new species, including the eventual evolution of **primates** and, much later, humans.

The Cambrian Explosion After the Great Dying

After the Permian extinction, life took millions of years to recover, but when it did, it led to the **Triassic Period**, a time when the first dinosaurs and mammals emerged. The extinction of dominant species, such as therapsids (mammal-like reptiles), created ecological opportunities for the diversification of reptiles, which eventually gave rise to the age of the dinosaurs. The evolutionary radiation that followed mass extinctions often leads to **adaptive radiations**, where surviving species rapidly evolve to fill the gaps left by those that perished.

Ecosystem Resilience

While mass extinctions are devastating, they also reveal the **resilience of life**. Ecosystems, though damaged, have the capacity to regenerate over long timescales. This resilience is evident in the fossil record, where periods of low biodiversity are followed by bursts of evolutionary innovation. The mass extinctions caused by tectonic upheavals, such as volcanic eruptions and the breakup of supercontinents, ultimately reshape the tree of life, pruning some branches while allowing others to grow in new directions.

Conclusion: The Dual Role of Tectonics in Life and Death

Plate tectonics, a fundamental force in shaping Earth's physical landscape, also plays a crucial role in life's evolutionary history. While tectonic activity can cause catastrophic mass extinctions through volcanic eruptions, climate changes, and the destruction of habitats, it also creates the conditions for new forms of life to emerge and thrive. The interplay between Earth's geology and biology is a dynamic and continuous process, demonstrating that life on Earth is not only shaped by natural selection but also by the powerful forces beneath our feet.

The mass extinctions caused by tectonic upheavals are reminders that life on Earth is fragile and that the forces that shape our planet can dramatically alter its trajectory. Yet, they also show that extinction is not the end of the story. In the aftermath of these events, life adapts, evolves, and rebounds, continuing the ever-changing narrative of our planet's deep history.

Chapter 8: Tectonics Beyond Earth – Searching for Life on Other Planets

The concept of plate tectonics is integral to understanding the Earth's dynamic systems, from the formation of continents and oceans to the regulation of its climate. This geological process, which continuously reshapes the planet's surface, has also had profound implications for the development and sustainability of life. On Earth, tectonic activity plays a critical role in the carbon cycle, which stabilizes the climate, and may have even created the conditions necessary for life to arise billions of years ago. But could tectonics also be a prerequisite for life on other planets? This chapter explores the search for tectonic activity on other planetary bodies, including Mars, Venus, and the icy moons of our solar system, such as Europa. We also examine the potential for tectonics on exoplanets—distant worlds orbiting stars outside our solar system—and what this could mean for the search for extraterrestrial life.

Mars and Venus: What Tectonic Evidence Tells Us About Their Potential for Life

Mars: A Frozen Desert with a Tectonic Past?

Mars, the fourth planet from the Sun, is often considered one of the most Earth-like planets in the solar system. For decades, scientists have been intrigued by Mars' surface features, which suggest that the planet once had active tectonic processes. While Mars does not exhibit the kind of plate tectonics that we see on Earth today, there is compelling evidence that tectonic activity may have occurred in its distant past.

One of the most striking features on Mars is the **Valles Marineris**, a canyon system that dwarfs the Grand Canyon on Earth. Stretching over 4,000 kilometers (2,500 miles), this vast chasm is believed to have formed through a combination of tectonic stretching and erosion. The rift-like nature of Valles Marineris suggests that Mars experienced tectonic forces early in its history, which caused the planet's crust to pull apart, possibly during periods of volcanic activity.

Another significant tectonic feature on Mars is the **Tharsis volcanic plateau**, a region that hosts some of the largest volcanoes in the solar system, including **Olympus Mons**, the tallest volcano and mountain on any planet. The formation of the Tharsis region is believed to have been driven by mantle plumes—columns of hot rock rising from deep within Mars' interior. These plumes likely created immense pressure on the planet's crust, causing it to deform and crack, which may have led to localized tectonic activity.

In terms of habitability, ancient tectonic activity on Mars could have had important implications. The volcanic eruptions associated with mantle plumes may have released gases such as water vapor, carbon dioxide, and methane into the atmosphere, creating a thicker, warmer environment that could have supported liquid water on the surface. Evidence from Mars' surface, including dried-up riverbeds and deltas, suggests that liquid water was once abundant. If tectonic processes contributed to this warm, wet period in Mars' history, it's possible that life could have emerged in ancient Martian lakes or underground aquifers.

While modern Mars is tectonically inactive, with a cold, thin atmosphere and no liquid water on its surface, scientists continue to study its geological history for clues about the planet's potential for past life. Future missions, such as the **ExoMars rover** and NASA's **Perseverance rover**, are equipped to search for signs of ancient life, focusing on areas where tectonic and volcanic activity might have created habitable environments.

Venus: A World of Catastrophic Resurfacing

Venus, often referred to as Earth's "sister planet" due to its similar size and composition, presents a vastly different geological and atmospheric picture. Unlike Earth, Venus is a scorching, hellish world with surface temperatures hot enough to melt lead and an atmosphere thick with carbon dioxide. However, beneath its thick veil of clouds, Venus shows evidence of intense tectonic and volcanic activity, though not in the form of plate tectonics like Earth.

One of the most puzzling aspects of Venus is the absence of tectonic plates. Instead, Venus appears to have experienced a process known as **catastrophic resurfacing**. Studies of Venus' surface using radar data from missions such as **Magellan** indicate that the planet's crust was likely subjected to massive volcanic eruptions and widespread tectonic deformation roughly 300 to 500 million years ago. This resurfacing event may have buried much of Venus' older geological history beneath layers of lava, erasing evidence of earlier tectonic activity.

Despite the lack of Earth-like plate tectonics, Venus shows signs of crustal deformation. The planet's surface is marked by large fault systems, mountain ranges, and rift valleys, suggesting that Venus' lithosphere experiences significant stress. Some scientists speculate that Venus might have a form of "episodic" tectonics, where heat builds up beneath the crust until it is released in massive, planet-wide convulsions. This contrasts sharply with Earth's continuous tectonic processes, where heat is released gradually through the movement of plates.

The tectonic history of Venus raises questions about its potential for habitability. While the current surface conditions on Venus are far too extreme for life as we know it, there is speculation that the planet may have been more Earth-like in its early history. Some climate models suggest that Venus might have had liquid water oceans and a more temperate climate before the runaway greenhouse effect took hold. If Venus once had tectonic processes that helped regulate its climate, it's possible that the planet could have supported life in its distant past. However, without more direct exploration of Venus' surface and subsurface, the true extent of its tectonic activity and its implications for life remain elusive.

Icy Moons: How Tectonics Might Operate on Moons Like Europa

Beyond the rocky planets, some of the most intriguing candidates for extraterrestrial life are found in the outer solar system, where icy moons orbit gas giants like Jupiter and Saturn. These moons, such as **Europa**, **Ganymede**, **Enceladus**, and **Titan**, have sparked scientific interest because they possess subsurface oceans beneath their icy crusts. Tectonic-like processes may play a key role in maintaining these oceans and potentially creating habitable environments.

Did Plate Tectonics Give Rise to Life?

Europa, one of Jupiter's largest moons, is a prime example of a celestial body where tectonic processes might foster life. Europa's surface is covered in a thick layer of ice, but beneath this ice, scientists believe there is a global ocean of liquid water. The surface of Europa is crisscrossed with cracks and ridges, which are thought to result from tectonic forces driven by **tidal flexing**. As Europa orbits Jupiter, the planet's immense gravity pulls on the moon, causing its icy shell to stretch and compress. This tidal flexing generates heat through friction, which could keep the subsurface ocean from freezing solid.

In addition to heat generation, Europa's tectonic activity may also allow for the exchange of materials between the icy surface and the ocean below. Some models suggest that cracks in Europa's ice could allow nutrients and organic molecules from the surface to mix with the ocean, creating a potentially habitable environment. Furthermore, evidence of water plumes erupting from Europa's surface, as observed by the **Hubble Space Telescope** and the **Galileo spacecraft**, hints at the possibility of liquid water reaching the surface through tectonic processes.

Enceladus, a smaller moon of Saturn, exhibits similar signs of tectonic activity. Like Europa, Enceladus has a subsurface ocean beneath its icy crust, and it has been observed ejecting water vapor and ice particles into space through geysers at its south pole. These geysers, driven by tidal forces from Saturn, suggest that tectonic processes could be actively shaping the moon's icy shell and maintaining its subsurface ocean. The presence of water, organic molecules, and heat make Enceladus a compelling candidate for the search for life.

Tectonics on icy moons like Europa and Enceladus provide a tantalizing glimpse into the potential for habitable environments beyond Earth. While these moons do not have plate tectonics in the traditional sense, their tidal flexing and cryovolcanism could create conditions similar to those found near hydrothermal vents on Earth—places where life thrives without sunlight, relying instead on chemical energy from the planet's interior.

Exoplanets: Could Tectonics Be a Requirement for Habitability on Distant Worlds?

As astronomers discover more and more **exoplanets**—planets orbiting stars outside our solar system—the search for life beyond Earth has expanded. One of the key questions is whether tectonic activity, like that found on Earth, is a necessary condition for a planet to support life.

On Earth, plate tectonics plays a crucial role in regulating the planet's climate and recycling essential elements, such as carbon, through the mantle and atmosphere. This process stabilizes the environment over geological timescales, preventing runaway greenhouse or icehouse conditions that could make the planet inhospitable. Could the same be true for exoplanets?

The discovery of potentially habitable exoplanets in the **habitable zone**—the region around a star where conditions are right for liquid water to exist—has raised hopes of finding life. However, being in the habitable zone alone may not be enough. Without tectonic activity to regulate the climate and recycle key elements, even a planet in the habitable zone could become inhospitable over time.

Some astronomers believe that tectonic activity might be a "goldilocks" condition for habitability. Planets that are too small may not have enough internal heat to drive tectonics, while planets that are too large might experience runaway volcanic activity. The right balance of size, composition, and distance from the star could determine whether tectonics—and thus life—can exist.

The search for tectonics on exoplanets is still in its early stages, but as technology advances, future telescopes and missions may be able to detect signs of geological activity on distant worlds. For now, Earth remains the only planet we know of with active plate tectonics, but the possibility of finding similar processes on other planets offers exciting prospects for the search for life in the universe.

In conclusion, the study of tectonic activity beyond Earth offers a fascinating avenue for understanding the potential for life on other planets and moons. While Mars and Venus show evidence of tectonic processes in the past, icy moons like Europa and Enceladus offer tantalizing clues about the possibility of habitable environments in the present. Looking further afield, the discovery of exoplanets raises the question of whether tectonics is a universal requirement for life. As we continue to explore our solar system and beyond, the search for tectonics will remain a key part of the quest to find extraterrestrial life.

Conclusion: Did Plate Tectonics Give Rise to Life?

The question of whether plate tectonics gave rise to life is one of the most profound and complex mysteries in Earth science. Throughout this book, we have explored the deep connections between the planet's geological processes and the emergence of life. While the full answer remains elusive, the evidence presented strongly suggests that Earth's unique tectonic activity played an indispensable role in creating and sustaining the conditions necessary for life to arise, evolve, and thrive.

To fully understand this question, it is essential to appreciate the intricate and multifaceted ways in which plate tectonics has shaped the Earth's environment over billions of years. These processes go far beyond the visible movements of continents and mountain building; they extend to the very foundations of Earth's atmosphere, hydrosphere, and biosphere. Plate tectonics is not just a geological phenomenon but a key driver of the Earth's long-term habitability.

1. Creating a Dynamic and Evolving Planet

One of the defining characteristics of Earth is its dynamic nature. Unlike other planets in our solar system, Earth's surface is constantly being reshaped by the movement of tectonic plates. This tectonic activity has played a critical role in the formation of continents, oceans, and other geological features. Without plate tectonics, Earth would likely resemble a stagnant, geologically inactive planet, much like Mars or Venus. This dynamic environment has been crucial for creating a planet capable of sustaining life.

The formation of Earth's early continents, driven by tectonic processes, provided a stable platform for the development of complex ecosystems. As continents moved, collided, and broke apart, new environments were created, leading to biodiversity and evolutionary innovation. For example, the creation of shallow seas along continental margins, rich in nutrients from tectonic uplift and erosion, may have been vital for the emergence of early life forms.

Moreover, plate tectonics constantly renews and recycles the Earth's surface. This recycling of the crust through subduction and volcanic activity plays a pivotal role in maintaining the Earth's habitability. Without it, the Earth's surface would have become sterile long ago, unable to support life. This recycling also contributes to long-term climate regulation, as we will explore further.

2. The Birth of the Atmosphere and Hydrosphere

Did Plate Tectonics Give Rise to Life?

The formation of Earth's atmosphere and oceans is inextricably linked to tectonic processes. In the early stages of Earth's history, volcanic outgassing, driven by tectonic forces, released vast quantities of water vapor, carbon dioxide, and other gases into the atmosphere. This process was critical in forming the early atmosphere and hydrosphere, laying the groundwork for life to emerge.

Plate tectonics also helped stabilize Earth's water cycle. As tectonic plates moved and formed new landmasses, they influenced the formation of oceans and seas. These bodies of water acted as a cradle for early life, providing the necessary medium for chemical reactions that could lead to the first living organisms. It is thought that Earth's unique combination of tectonic activity and liquid water may be one of the key factors that distinguishes it from other planets in the solar system and beyond.

Additionally, tectonic activity plays an ongoing role in maintaining the stability of Earth's climate and oceans. Subduction zones, where oceanic plates are pushed into the mantle and recycled, help regulate the levels of gases like carbon dioxide in the atmosphere, which has a direct impact on global temperatures. Without this regulation, Earth's climate could have spiraled into extremes, either freezing over or becoming unbearably hot, making life as we know it impossible.

3. Hydrothermal Vents and the Origin of Life

Perhaps one of the most compelling pieces of evidence linking plate tectonics to the origin of life is the existence of hydrothermal vents. These deep-sea ecosystems, found along mid-ocean ridges where tectonic plates diverge, provide a unique environment where life can thrive without sunlight. Hydrothermal vents release chemically rich fluids from within the Earth, creating conditions that may resemble those in which life first emerged.

The discovery of extremophiles—organisms that thrive in the harsh conditions of these vents—has revolutionized our understanding of life's potential origins. These organisms rely on chemosynthesis, using chemical energy from the Earth's interior rather than sunlight to sustain themselves. This has led to the hypothesis that life could have originated around such vents, where tectonic activity created an energy-rich, chemically diverse environment.

In the early Earth, when the planet's surface was likely too hostile for life due to intense radiation and frequent impacts from space debris, deep-sea hydrothermal vents may have provided a sanctuary for the first simple life forms. The heat and minerals released by these vents, along with the protection from harmful solar radiation offered by the ocean, could have created the perfect incubator for life to take root. This environment, driven by tectonic activity, may have been essential in sparking the transition from non-living chemicals to living organisms.

4. Long-Term Climate Stability and the Evolution of Life

One of the most critical roles of plate tectonics in the story of life is its regulation of Earth's climate over geological timescales. The carbon-silicate cycle, which governs the long-term balance of carbon dioxide in the atmosphere, is directly influenced by tectonic processes. Volcanic activity, driven by plate movements, releases carbon dioxide into the atmosphere, while the weathering of silicate rocks (which are formed as a result of tectonic uplift) removes carbon dioxide, storing it in rocks and the ocean floor.

This delicate balance between carbon release and sequestration has helped regulate Earth's temperature for billions of years, preventing the planet from entering a runaway greenhouse effect or freezing over entirely. Without plate tectonics, this self-regulating system would not exist, and Earth's climate could have become too unstable to support life for long periods.

Mass extinctions, triggered in part by tectonic upheavals such as massive volcanic eruptions, have periodically reset the evolutionary clock. These catastrophic events, while devastating, also create opportunities for new life forms to evolve and flourish in the aftermath. The rise of mammals after the extinction of the dinosaurs is one such example. Tectonic activity, by shaping the planet's physical and climatic environment, has been a key driver of both extinction and evolution.

5. Life as a Geological Force

While plate tectonics has shaped life, life itself has also shaped the planet's geology. The evolution of photosynthetic organisms transformed the atmosphere, introducing oxygen, which in turn influenced the types of minerals and rocks that could form. This interplay between life and geology underscores the idea that Earth is not just a passive environment for life but an active participant in its evolution.

As life evolved and became more complex, it influenced erosion, sedimentation, and even the carbon cycle. Plants, for example, accelerated the weathering of rocks, releasing nutrients into the soil and oceans, which in turn supported more life. This feedback loop between the biosphere and the geosphere highlights the co-evolution of Earth's geology and biology, with plate tectonics at the center of this dynamic relationship.

Final Thoughts: The Role of Plate Tectonics in Life's Grand Story

Did Plate Tectonics Give Rise to Life?

While the full answer to whether plate tectonics gave rise to life may remain unknown, the evidence strongly suggests that Earth's unique tectonic processes created the essential conditions for life to not only emerge but to thrive. Plate tectonics provided the right environmental niches, regulated the planet's atmosphere and climate, and continuously reshaped the surface to foster biodiversity and evolutionary innovation.

In the search for life beyond Earth, one of the key questions scientists ask is whether other planets exhibit tectonic activity similar to Earth's. This connection between tectonics and habitability raises exciting possibilities for discovering life on planets with active geology, both in our solar system and beyond.

In the end, plate tectonics may be one of the fundamental processes that make Earth a living planet, and it may hold the key to understanding life's deepest mysteries—not just on Earth but throughout the universe.

Glossary

A

- **Abiogenesis**: The process by which life arises naturally from non-living matter, typically under conditions present on early Earth. This concept is central to theories of life's origin in environments like hydrothermal vents.
- **Atmosphere**: The layer of gases surrounding a planet. Earth's atmosphere consists of nitrogen, oxygen, carbon dioxide, and other gases that were significantly influenced by volcanic activity, which is linked to plate tectonics.

B

- **Black Smokers**: A type of hydrothermal vent found on the ocean floor, releasing superheated water rich in minerals, which may have provided the conditions for life to originate.
- **Biogeochemical Cycle**: The movement of elements like carbon, nitrogen, and oxygen through Earth's systems—biosphere, atmosphere, hydrosphere, and lithosphere—often influenced by both biological processes and geological activity.

C

- **Carbon Cycle**: The process by which carbon is exchanged between the atmosphere, oceans, soil, and living organisms. Plate tectonics influences the cycle by driving volcanic eruptions, which release carbon dioxide into the atmosphere.
- **Continental Drift**: The gradual movement of Earth's continents across the ocean floor due to tectonic forces. The concept was first proposed by Alfred Wegener and later integrated into the theory of plate tectonics.

D

- **Divergent Boundary**: A type of tectonic plate boundary where two plates move away from each other, often resulting in the formation of mid-ocean ridges, volcanic activity, and the creation of new oceanic crust.
- **Deep Time**: A term used to describe the vast span of Earth's geological history, which extends over billions of years and is central to understanding the long processes that allowed for the emergence of life.

E

- **Erosion**: The process by which rocks are broken down by weathering agents like water, wind, and biological activity. Erosion, influenced by plate

Did Plate Tectonics Give Rise to Life?
tectonics and biological processes, shapes Earth's landscape.

- **Endosymbiosis**: A theory in biology suggesting that some organelles in eukaryotic cells, such as mitochondria, originated as free-living bacteria that were engulfed by ancestral cells, possibly as a result of tectonic-driven environmental shifts.

F

- **Feedback Loop**: A process in which the output of a system feeds back into the system to influence its future behavior. In terms of plate tectonics and life, tectonic processes can create environmental changes that affect life, which in turn influences geological processes.
- **Fossil Record**: The preserved remains or traces of ancient life found in rock layers. Studying the fossil record helps scientists understand the evolution of life in relation to Earth's geological changes.

G

- **Geochemical Energy**: Energy derived from chemical reactions, such as those occurring at hydrothermal vents, that may have been crucial for the development of life in Earth's early oceans.
- **Geological Time Scale**: A system of chronological dating that divides Earth's history into eons, eras,

periods, and epochs, helping to map the evolution of life in relation to tectonic events.

H

- **Hydrothermal Vents**: Fissures in the Earth's crust from which geothermally heated water rich in minerals flows into the ocean. These vents are thought to have provided the necessary conditions for early life to develop.
- **Hotspots**: Areas of the Earth's mantle that are unusually hot, often creating volcanic activity on the surface as a plate moves over them, such as the Hawaiian Islands. Hotspots are an example of how tectonic processes create dynamic environments for life.

I

- **Isostasy**: The equilibrium between Earth's lithosphere and asthenosphere, where the crust "floats" on the denser mantle beneath it. This principle helps explain the vertical motion of Earth's continents over geological time.
- **Icehouse Earth**: A period of Earth's history characterized by cooler global temperatures and widespread ice cover, which was influenced by changes in tectonic activity, particularly the arrangement of continents and ocean currents.

J

- **Jovian Planets**: A term for the gas giants (Jupiter, Saturn, Uranus, and Neptune). While not directly related to Earth's tectonics, these planets provide insight into the formation and evolution of planetary bodies, contrasting with the tectonic dynamics on Earth.

L

- **Lithosphere**: The rigid outer layer of the Earth, composed of the crust and the uppermost part of the mantle. The lithosphere is broken into tectonic plates, which float on the more fluid asthenosphere beneath.
- **Lava**: Molten rock that erupts from a volcano, often created by tectonic processes at divergent or convergent boundaries. Lava can contribute to the formation of new landmasses.

M

- **Mantle Convection**: The process by which heat from Earth's interior causes the mantle to flow, driving the movement of tectonic plates. This process is fundamental to plate tectonics and affects Earth's surface features.

- **Mid-Ocean Ridge**: A vast underwater mountain range formed by divergent tectonic plate boundaries, where new oceanic crust is created, which could have influenced the development of early life.

N

- **Neoproterozoic Era**: A geological period that predates the Cambrian explosion, which saw major tectonic shifts, including the break-up of the supercontinent Rodinia, which influenced Earth's climate and biological evolution.

O

- **Oceanic Crust**: The Earth's crust beneath the oceans, which is thinner and denser than continental crust. The formation and subduction of oceanic crust are key to the recycling of Earth's surface material.
- **Orogeny**: The process of mountain formation, often associated with tectonic plate collision and subduction. The Himalayas, for example, were formed by the collision of the Indian and Eurasian plates.

P

- **Plate Tectonics**: The scientific theory explaining the movement of Earth's lithospheric plates, which causes the formation of continents, ocean basins, earthquakes, and volcanic activity. Plate tectonics is a driving force behind geological and biological changes on Earth.

- **Pangaea**: A supercontinent that existed during the late Paleozoic and early Mesozoic eras, formed by the convergence of Earth's landmasses. The breakup of Pangaea due to plate tectonics had a profound effect on global climate and biodiversity.

- **Paleomagnetism**: The study of Earth's ancient magnetic field preserved in rocks. By examining the orientation of magnetic minerals in rock strata, scientists can trace the movement of tectonic plates over time.

R

- **Rift Valley**: A type of tectonic boundary where a continent is splitting apart due to divergent plate movement. The East African Rift is an example where tectonic forces are pulling the land apart, potentially creating new habitats.

- **Radiation**: The release of energy in the form of electromagnetic waves or particles. Plate tectonics indirectly influences radiation on Earth through volcanic activity and the atmosphere's role in protecting life from solar radiation.

S

- **Subduction Zone**: A tectonic boundary where one plate is forced beneath another, often leading to the formation of deep ocean trenches, volcanic arcs, and mountain ranges. Subduction zones are also sites of significant geological activity that can affect life on Earth.
- **Supervolcano**: A large volcano capable of producing an eruption of a magnitude far greater than typical volcanic events. Supervolcanic eruptions can dramatically alter Earth's atmosphere and climate.

T

- **Tectonic Plates**: Large, rigid segments of Earth's lithosphere that float atop the more fluid asthenosphere. Their movements are responsible for the formation of continents, mountains, and ocean basins, and they play a critical role in Earth's geology.
- **Tectonic Uplift**: The rising of Earth's crust, typically caused by tectonic forces at convergent plate boundaries, which can create mountain ranges and influence local climate and ecosystems.

V

- **Volcanic Outgassing**: The release of gases from Earth's interior through volcanic activity. These gases, such as carbon dioxide, water vapor, and sulfur dioxide, have contributed to the development of Earth's early atmosphere and oceans.

W

- **Water Cycle**: The continuous movement of water within Earth's hydrosphere, including processes like evaporation, precipitation, and infiltration. Plate tectonics influences the cycle by shaping oceans and continents, impacting global climate and ecosystems.

Bibliography

1. "The Earth: A Very Short Introduction" by Martin Redfern

A concise and accessible overview of Earth's history, including the processes that shaped its structure and atmosphere. Perfect for building the foundational knowledge about Earth's geology.

2. "The Origin of Continents and Oceans" by Alfred Wegener

This classic work introduces the theory of continental drift, which laid the groundwork for the modern understanding of plate tectonics. Wegener's pioneering ideas are essential for understanding the geological forces that shaped Earth.

3. "The Dynamic Earth: An Introduction to Physical Geology" by Brian J. Skinner and Stephen C. Porter

This textbook provides a solid understanding of Earth's physical geology, including the theory of plate tectonics, earthquakes, volcanoes, and the evolution of Earth's surface. It's a must-read for grasping the scientific foundations of your book.

4. "The Hot Earth: The Geology of the Early Earth" by Michael Wysession

Explores the history of the early Earth and the role of tectonic processes in shaping the planet's surface, atmosphere, and potential for life. It will provide critical context on how tectonics could have influenced the emergence of life.

5. "Life on a Young Planet: The First Three Billion Years of Evolution on Earth" by Andrew H. Knoll

This book focuses on the conditions that allowed life to arise on Earth, including the environmental and geological factors such as plate tectonics. Knoll's exploration of early Earth's environments is crucial for understanding the relationship between geology and life.

6. "The Volcano Adventure Guide" by Rosaly M. C. Lopes

While focusing on volcanoes, this guide explains the role of volcanic activity (often associated with plate tectonics) in shaping Earth's geology and influencing life, particularly early life forms.

7. "The Earth System" by Lee R. Kump, James F. Kasting, and Robert G. Crane

This textbook offers a comprehensive look at the interactions between Earth's physical, chemical, and biological systems. It discusses how plate tectonics is deeply connected to Earth's climate and biogeochemical cycles, vital for understanding how tectonics and life are intertwined.

8. "Astrobiology: A Very Short Introduction" by David C. Catling

This book looks at the conditions required for life to exist elsewhere in the universe, including the importance of planetary geology. It also explores how Earth's tectonic processes could have influenced life's origins, making it a perfect complement to your exploration of life's deep origins.

Acknowledgments

Writing *Did Plate Tectonics Give Rise to Life? Unraveling Earth's Deepest Mystery* has been an incredible journey, one made possible by the support, insights, and encouragement of many individuals. I would like to express my deepest gratitude to all those who have helped bring this book to life.

First and foremost, I must thank the scientific community, whose work has been a continuous source of inspiration throughout my research. I am especially grateful to the geologists, biologists, and astrobiologists whose groundbreaking studies have deepened our understanding of Earth's complex systems and the profound connection between geology and life. The works of scientists such as Alfred Wegener, J. Tuzo Wilson, and more recently, those in the field of deep-sea hydrothermal research, have been invaluable in shaping this book.

I also owe a great debt of thanks to my research assistants, who helped sift through countless papers, articles, and textbooks. Their dedication to gathering and organizing information allowed me to focus on the larger narrative. A special mention goes to my assistant, who provided expertise in plate tectonics and atmospheric sciences that greatly enhanced the accuracy and depth of this work.

To my editor, your keen eye for detail, thoughtful suggestions, and unwavering support have made this book far better than I could have ever imagined. Your guidance was indispensable throughout the editing process, and your ability to transform complex scientific concepts into accessible, engaging prose has truly shaped this book into something special.

I would like to thank my family and friends for their endless support and patience during this long process. Your belief in me and this project kept me motivated, even during the most challenging times. A particular thank you to my son Abdullah, who offered constructive feedback and always reminded me to stay true to my passion for sharing knowledge with others.

Lastly, to the readers—whether you are a student, a scientist, or simply someone curious about the mysteries of our planet—thank you for your interest in this topic. It is my hope that this book will spark your curiosity, ignite your imagination, and deepen your appreciation for the intricate and awe-inspiring forces that shape our Earth.

This book is a tribute to the endless curiosity that drives us to understand the world around us, and I am eternally grateful for all the people who have made it possible.

Thank you.

Sincerely,

Zahid Ameer
Versatile Indie Author

Disclaimer:

The information presented in this book, *Did Plate Tectonics Give Rise to Life? Unraveling Earth's Deepest Mystery*, is based on current scientific knowledge and research at the time of publication. While every effort has been made to ensure accuracy, the field of geology and the study of life's origins are constantly evolving. New discoveries, theories, and interpretations may emerge that could alter or refine the understanding of the topics discussed in this book.

This book is intended for educational and informational purposes only. The author and publisher do not claim to offer definitive answers to the complex questions surrounding the relationship between plate tectonics and the origin of life. Readers are encouraged to explore further research and consult professional experts in the fields of geology, biology, and other relevant sciences.

The views expressed in this book are those of the author and do not necessarily reflect the opinions of any institution or organization mentioned. Any references to scientific studies or data sources are meant to provide context and stimulate further exploration, and are not intended to be comprehensive or exhaustive.

About me

I am Zahid Ameer, hailing from the vibrant country of India. As an author, ghostwriter, bibliophile, online affiliate marketer, blogger, YouTuber, graphic designer, and animal lover, I have woven my passions into a unique tapestry that defines my life's work.

Born and raised in India, I have always possessed a deep love for literature. With an insatiable appetite for books, I have amassed an impressive collection of around 1,600 titles, predominantly in English. My passion for reading brings me immense joy and serves as a source of inspiration for my writing endeavors.

I have compiled an impressive portfolio of written works as an author and ghostwriter. With a captivating writing style and an innate ability to craft engaging narratives, I bring my stories to life, captivating readers from all walks of life. My wide range of interests and experiences contribute to the richness of my writing, allowing me to connect with my audience on a heartfelt level effortlessly.

Beyond my literary pursuits, I have also established a strong presence on various digital platforms. I utilize my YouTube channel and blog to raise awareness about all types of knowledge and to share heartwarming stories of animals. Using my platform to shed light on important issues, I strive to create a world where humans and animals can coexist harmoniously.

In addition to my work as an author, I have also dabbled in the world of affiliate marketing. With my webpreneur spirit, I have ventured into online marketing, leveraging my knowledge and skills to promote products and services that align with my values.

However, my most cherished role is that of a father. Family is at the core of my being, and everything I do is centered around creating a better future for my loved ones. My dedication to my family is evident in my passion for personal growth and my relentless pursuit of success. Through my various endeavors, I strive to set an example of perseverance and ambition for my children, inspiring them to chase their dreams unapologetically.

In a world where specialization often dominates, I defy convention by embracing multiple passions and excelling in diverse fields. My love for books, animals, and family has become the driving force behind my achievements. By the grace of Almighty God, my unique blend of characteristics has allowed me to leave an indelible mark on the world, enriching the lives of those I encounter along the way.

To your grand success in life,

Zahid Ameer
Versatile Indie Author